The Design Patterns Companion

Scott L. Bain

Library of Congress Cataloging-in-Publication Data has been applied for.

ISBN: 978-1-62825-658-1

Published by: Project Management Institute, Inc.
                14 Campus Boulevard
                Newtown Square, Pennsylvania 19073-3299 USA
                Phone: +1 610 356 4600
                Fax: +1 610 356 4647
                Email: customercare@pmi.org
                Internet: www.PMI.org

To place a Trade Order or for pricing information, please contact Independent Publishers Group:
Independent Publishers Group
Order Department
814 North Franklin Street
Chicago, IL 60610 USA
Phone: +1 800 888 4741
Fax: +1 312 337 5985
Email: orders@ipgbook.com (For orders only)

For all other inquiries, please contact the PMI Book Service Center.
PMI Book Service Center
P.O. Box 932683, Atlanta, GA 31193-2683 USA
Phone: +1 866 276 4764 (within the U.S. or Canada) or +1 770 280 4129 (globally)
Fax: +1 770 280 4113
Email: info@bookorders.pmi.org

10 9 8 7 6 5 4 3 2 1

Table of Contents

Introduction From the Author

Design patterns were originally delineated in the seminal work of the "Gang of Four": Erich Gamma, Richard Helm, Ralph Johnson, and John Vlissides. They, in turn, were responding to an earlier work by the architect Christopher Alexander, *The Timeless Way of Building*. The Gang of Four's work, *Design Patterns: Elements of Reusable Object-Oriented Software*, received a lot of attention when it was originally published in 1994.

Some have suggested, however, that the industry has moved beyond the patterns in the more than two decades that have passed since its publication, and that in the age of agile processes and test-driven development, the patterns are no longer relevant. They say that patterns represent an old view, namely "big design up front."

I disagree. Not only do I think the patterns are relevant today, I believe they are far more relevant than they were when the work was originally published. Here's why:

Patterns form a rich language of design. This is all the more important now that nearly all software projects are highly collaborative. We need reliable ways to communicate and make group decisions. Nearly all complex human activity involves specialized language: medicine, law, engineering, etc. They all have their own rich nomenclature to describe what is being proposed, or what has been done.

Patterns all follow the principles of good design in different ways. This means they are highly changeable without decay. The agile movement says, among other things, that we must embrace change. The patterns help us to do this.

This book is not meant to teach you the patterns; see the References section for books that do. This is meant to be a field guide for those who are already pattern practitioners, something to refer to as part of your day-to-day activities.

What Design Patterns Represent

The Design Patterns movement, begun (in software) by the Gang of Four (GoF) (Gamma, Helm, Johnson, & Vlissides, 1994), essentially elevated certain design elements as valuable, repeated, and high-quality examples of a particular approach to design.

Their general advice was given in three parts:

1. Design to interfaces.
2. Favor composition over inheritance.
3. Encapsulate the concept that varies.

All patterns adhere to this rubric in different ways. But they also all exhibit certain qualities of design, and they all adhere to a set of shared principles. What I will outline in the following pages are the three bits of guidance listed above, as well as how each pattern respects:

- Strong cohesion
- Proper coupling
- Robust encapsulation
- Avoiding redundancy
- Testability

In addition, I will submit that each pattern follows good principles in design, such as open-closed, the separation of concerns, and others.

I'll start with the definitions, then examine the patterns.

Design to Interfaces

Behavior in object-oriented systems is a reflection of the interaction of objects. If you change the objects or alter their interactions, the resulting behavior changes.

This means that objects have relationships to other objects, usually through references that are used to call methods. The GoF recommends that these relationships are defined based on how the objects look to each other, not by how the objects are implemented.

It's easy to misinterpret this to mean "every object should have a separate interface," referring to the type "interface" that many languages provide. But the advice was not meant to indicate any language-specific idiom.

An "interface" means any defined means of communication. A method signature is an interface; the collective public methods of a class are an interface; an abstract class is an interface; etc. What is meant by that is the interface of any interaction should be based on what is needed by the clients and not the way the behavior is implemented. Changing the implementation should not affect the interface, and thus should not affect the clients.

In other words, the full version of this is "design to interfaces (how you work with them) rather than implementations (what each actually does)."

Favor Composition Over Inheritance

Composition/aggregation indicates a "has-a" relationship between objects. Inheritance, on the other hand, indicates an "is-a" relationship. The GoF would seem to be suggesting that you lean toward ("favor") the former rather than the latter.

The potentially confusing aspect of this is that the patterns they delineate in the book use inheritance fairly extensively. Why would they recommend against this, and then do it?

Inheritance can be used for two different things:

1. To create polymorphism: Subclasses can be exchanged for each other, and can be cast to their base type, hiding their actual type from clients.
2. To specialize: Subclasses gain elements from their base class that they can accept or change, creating special versions of whatever the base class does.

What the advice means is that we should shy away from doing the latter, for the most part. If you examine the patterns, you'll see that inheritance is almost always used as a way of creating interchangeability through polymorphism.

This was also meant to disabuse designers from the notion that inheritance is for reuse. Reuse, it says, is better achieved using delegation through an interface, rather than the more intimate connection that inheritance-for-specialization creates.

Encapsulate the Concept That Varies

The full text of this advice is (Gamma et al., 1994):

> "Consider what should be variable in your design and encapsulate the concept that varies."

To a modern agile developer, the word "should" is a bit of a red flag. It presumes that we know, ahead of time, what is going to change. We don't believe this, and we certainly don't want to depend on guessing correctly.

It is good to remember that the book precedes the agile movement and, in this regard, perhaps reflects an old point of view. But the advice is not obsolete, it just needs a bit of an update. It should say:

> Consider what *has become* variable in your design and encapsulate the concept that varies.

We don't predict; we react. But what does it mean to encapsulate a concept that varies? Many things can vary in software, such as behavior, the cardinality of relationships, the sequence/workflow of an interaction, the specific design of a subsystem, and the way objects are created and/or stored.

Encapsulation does not simply mean "making things private." Instead, it means hiding of any kind, of anything. What you hide, you can change. So, the advice really means "*hide all variations*."

As we examine the patterns, we will see that each one hides different variations from the rest of the system, reducing the cost and impact of changing them as requirements change.

Qualities, Principles, Practices

I'm going to be using these terms quite a bit, so it might be useful to explain how I am using them, just for the sake of clarity.

By **quality**, I am referring to an aspect of design that is desirable or, if missing, is a deficit. In general, the qualities I look for make it easier to change things, since maintenance is the major expense in most systems.

By **principle**, I mean general guidance about design, concepts that can inform our decisions in many different ways depending on circumstances. Principles are almost never perfectly achievable, but they are always important to keep in mind. The Golden Rule is a principle that we try to follow in polite society. Do we follow it all the time? No, but we try to as much as possible. That's the sort of thing I mean.

By **practice**, I am referring to actions we take which have been accepted as universally good. Doctors always clean their hands and instruments. Carpenters always measure twice before they cut. Lawyers always preserve all documents. Software has these "always" actions as well, and I want to examine/promote a few.

I will start with the qualities that all patterns share, then the principles they follow. Then after I write about the patterns themselves, I will cover some good practices that they promote.

Qualities Patterns Share: Strong Cohesion

Cohesion is a quality-indicting alignment. The best way to understand and remember this is to relate the root word "cohere" to the term *coherent*. Lasers are often called *coherent light* because all the beams of light in a laser are perfectly aligned.

What does this mean in software? It has to do with scoping, and we focus on two versions of creating scope: class scope and method scope.

Classes create their own scope. If they are strongly cohesive, then everything within the scope of a class is aligned in that **all the contents of a class are about fulfilling the class's single responsibility.**

Methods create their own scope as well, but in this case the alignment is about function. **All elements of a method should be aligned in that they are about performing the same, single function.**

No red herrings. No 20-page methods. No grab-bag classes. Everything is focused and aligned and, therefore, coherent.

Getting this right can sometimes be tricky. The practices we follow can be helpful here. When we get to the practices, I'll be able to show how following them can ensure we produce strong cohesion in design whether a pattern is involved or not.

Qualities Patterns Share: Proper Coupling

Coupling can be said to exist when one part of a system is impacted by changes to another part. Where there is too much of this, changes to a system can be difficult, time consuming, and potentially destructive.

That said, coupling is also necessary. When objects collaborate with each other then they must interact, and this always creates some form of coupling among them.

Given that coupling is both needed and can be problematic, this means that there is both good and bad coupling in a system.

"Loose" is the term most people use when they think the coupling is the way it should be. I prefer the term "intentional" because it means the coupling was created on purpose to achieve a goal, and will therefore make sense and be expected to exist. Developers are smart; they never intend bad or excessive coupling.

"Tight" is the term people use to describe poor or excessive coupling, but I prefer the term "accidental." The coupling we don't want is the coupling we never intended in the first place, but we sometimes make mistakes. When we discover coupling that exists but serves no defined purpose, then we seek to find a way to eliminate it.

Here, again, the patterns will help us. All the coupling in every pattern is there for a defined reason, is logical and meaningful, and is therefore intentional.

Qualities Patterns Share: Avoiding Redundancy

Redundancy can be a good thing if we are referring to a backup for safety, like the systems on a spacecraft. I don't mean that kind of redundancy. I am referring instead to an element of the system that is repeated needlessly in such a way that altering it will require the same change to be performed multiple times.

A good example of making such a mistake is the Y2K bug. Remediating for the Y2K situation was not expensive because changing from a two-digit date to a four-digit date is inherently difficult. It was expensive because we had to make that same change millions of times. We knew it would be easy to miss some, and so we had to proceed very slowly and methodically. Y2K remediation produced little or no business value, but cost billions of dollars.

This bug was created at a time when the expensive part of automating something was the hardware. Memory, disk space, and computing cycles were all very costly and also very limited in terms of what was even possible. The human programmer was seen as a fairly trivial expense.

Today, this equation is reversed. Developers are expensive, but computer hardware is cheap and getting cheaper all the time. Redundancies cost more in developer time.

Any change should be able to be made in a single place. The patterns will help us to enforce this in various ways, as we shall see.

Qualities Patterns Share: Robust Encapsulation

Much of the literature on object orientation defines encapsulation as "data hiding." While this is true, it is far too limited as a definition. Data hiding is encapsulation. Not all encapsulation is data hiding.

Encapsulation is the hiding of anything. Here are some examples:

- Interfaces, abstract classes, and concrete base classes can be used to hide the types of classes that implement or derive from them, by casting.

- Factories can encapsulate the specific design of a subsystem; clients call the factory but do not couple to the specific details of what is built.

- The number of entities in a collaboration (cardinality) can be hidden. All clients see a single interaction when, in fact, there may be more.

- Workflows and the details of interactions that vary by circumstance can be hidden.

- Whether an instance is shared or not can be hidden.

Whenever something can be hidden, you gain advantages if you have to change it. You have much greater freedom when you can make a change without extensively investigating the system, without fear that you may introduce a defect, and without, in fact, creating one.

What you hide you can freely change. Each pattern hides different things from the rest of the system.

Qualities Patterns Share: Testability

All software should ideally be tested. That said, some designs are more easily tested than others. This "testability" factor can be very useful in determining the quality of a given design, because:

1. When a design is excessively coupled, then testing any class in it will require that many other parts of the system are created in the test. This can make tests complex to write and slow to run. The test will also fail for multiple reasons.

2. When a class has multiple responsibilities (weak cohesion), then those responsibilities must be tested together. The tests become difficult to read, write, and maintain.

3. When the system has redundancies, the tests will also because the same issues will have to be tested repeatedly.

4. When encapsulation is weak, many side effects are possible, and thus tests must be written to guard against them. The test suite becomes many times larger than the production package or namespace.

Testability, therefore, is really the quality of all qualities because weakness in design always makes testing difficult and painful. Pain is, after all, nature's diagnostic tool. We feel pain in order to know that something is wrong.

The earlier that testability is considered, the earlier design flaws can be discovered and corrected.

Principles Patterns Follow: Open-Closed

Bertrand Meyer (1988), based on an idea put forth earlier by Ivar Jacobsen, said, "Software entities (classes, modules, functions, etc.) should be **open** for extension, but **closed** to modification."

What does this mean? It means that one aspect of strong design is that it allows new functions, features, behaviors, etc., to be **added** to a system in such a way that the previously existing code does not have to be **altered**.

Most experienced developers will tell you they would much prefer to make something new rather than change something old. This is because they have experienced both things and have found that making new things is less difficult, less dangerous, less time consuming, and, in general, is something they feel more confident about doing.

How can this principle be achieved? You can make a system open-closed in many different ways, depending on what you want to be able to add later by cleanly plugging in a new entity. The entity can be anything: a class, a method, a delegate, a mix-in, etc.

Each design pattern follows open-closed in a different way, about a different thing or set of things. They are various examples of *componentization*.

Understanding this is an interesting way to distinguish each pattern from the others. We will examine this aspect of each pattern as we explore it.

Principles Patterns Follow: Liskov Substitution

Barbara Liskov's (1994) research showed that clients that use base classes must be able to use objects of derived classes without changing.

When a class is derived from a base class, we traditionally call this an "is-a" relationship. But Liskov suggests that we should instead consider it to be a "behaves-like" relationship and, when this determined to be untrue, then perhaps inheritance is being misused.

One place where I saw this in action was in a scheduling system. The system began with the concept of an "event," which had a start date, end date, start time, and end time.

Later, a "daylong event" was added by subclassing "event," since a "daylong event *is an* event." However, the "daylong event" was altered such that the start and end times were locked at midnight to midnight, since a "day is a 24-hour period."

This caused problems when support for different time zones was added. Daylong events that were 12:00 a.m. to 12:00 a.m. in one time zone were 9:00 p.m. to 9:00 p.m. in others, spanning two actual days.

This time-zone adjustment worked properly for "events," but did not work for "daylong events" because a 24-hour period is not always a day, but often involves two days; they did not "behave" the same way and, therefore, were not substitutable.

The abstraction should have been "event," with two separate implementations: "daylong event" and "timed event." There should have been no inheritance relationship between them. The patterns operate this way.

Principles Patterns Follow: Dependency Inversion

Robert Martin (2003) said, "High-level modules should not depend on low-level modules; both should depend on abstractions. Abstractions should not depend on details. Details should depend upon abstractions."

When objects interact, they do so through some kind of interface. An interface is always an abstraction of some kind. The first part of this principle is about making sure these abstractions are not tied to specific implementations.

But there is more to consider. How is an interface created? Based on what? What should the methods of a service look like, and what should the signatures of those methods be?

In both cases, we should avoid basing an interface on how the entity functions (its implementation). Rather, it should be based on how it will be used (the conceptual, or abstract view of the behavior in question).

Test-first promotes this because the first time an interface is accessed, it is by the test and also before the implementation has been created. The influence must be from use. The test is the first user/client of the behavior.

The patterns all also display this kind of dependency inversion, and therefore each is an example of why this principle is so crucial in keeping systems cleanly maintainable.

Principles Patterns Follow: Separation of Concerns

Good design separates things that change for independent reasons. This is often called the "separation of concerns" (Dijkstra, 1982) and applies to many different aspects of design, process, and analysis.

Below are some examples of aspects of an entity that should ideally be handled separately from one another.

- The conceptual aspect: What it is.
- The specification aspect: How to use it.
- The implementation aspect: How it works.
- The creation aspect: How it is made.
- The selection aspect: How it is chosen.
- The workflow view: How it collaborates.

Therefore:

The factory for an entity should make it *but not use it*.

The clients to an entity should use it *but not make it*.

Entities should be able to couple to each other conceptually, *without also doing so concretely*.

Two entities should be able to interact in *different ways* with the same third entity.

By "entity," I mean class, method, function, subsystem, anything that creates behavior in a system.

Patterns separate concerns in various ways, depending on what the concerns are.

The Patterns Themselves

The next series of pages will be about the patterns themselves. For each pattern, there will be two (facing) pages, and I will delineate for each pattern:

- The kind of domain issue the pattern applies to;
- A concrete and/or conceptual example of the pattern with a UML diagram or diagrams;
- How the pattern displays/exemplifies the qualities and principles of good design;
- How to unit test the pattern;
- Some caveats, questions, decisions, and concerns about the pattern; and
- Other patterns that often accompany this one.

Not all of these patterns come from the Gang of Four book, and I will not cover all the patterns that do.

This is a set of patterns that I personally believe every developer should know, and which I believe are the best ones to study if you want to understand patterns overall and the kind of design they promote.

Not all good designs are patterns. But all designs should be as good as the patterns are. By studying the patterns, you are also studying good design.

These are **brief conceptual sketches** of the patterns to quickly remind you of the details of each one. A link to a more thorough discussion will also be provided in each case, using the PMI Pattern Repository.

The Abstract Factory

Intent: Create an interface for creating sets of dependent or related instances that implement a set of abstract types.

The *abstract factory* coordinates the instantiation of sets of objects that have varying implementations in such a way that only legitimate combinations of instances are ever created.

Example: If an application is to be deployed on a variety of operating systems, it will need the "right one" of a number of different drivers: memory access, keyboard, mouse, file system, display, sound, etc. The right set of drivers for Windows will be different from that set of drivers for Linux, and yet different from those for OSX. Under no circumstances should a Windows display driver be used alongside a Linux memory manager, etc. Drivers "go together;" they are a *family*.

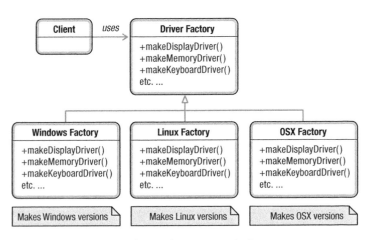

Figure 1: Abstract factory example diagram.

Qualities and Principles: Each version of the factory is concerned with implementations for one case only. All client code couples solely to abstractions. Any otherwise-redundant implementation of the factories can be moved to the base class. Clients do not couple to concrete services, nor are they exposed to the number of cases there are, nor which one they are currently using, creating open-closedness on all of these issues. All factories are substitutable for each other.

Testing: Each concrete factory can be tested on its own to ensure it builds the correct set of objects. The test would call each "make" method and type-check what it produces to ensure it is the class intended.

Questions and Concerns: The pattern does not specify how the proper factory is determined and created because there are many different ways to accomplish this, including another factory.

Supporting an entirely new kind of service will cause all factories and clients to be changed; if, in the example, we realized late in the day that we need a driver for touchscreens in each operating system, this will cause sweeping maintenance across the system.

Note that this is not a "failure" of the pattern; it reveals a lapse in the requirements analysis process that would have ultimately caused this problem anyway. Patterns lend clarity to such issues; they do not create them.

For more information: https://tinyurl.com/y5q7ayzm

The Adapter

Intent: Convert the interface of a class into another interface clients expect. The *adapter* lets classes work together that couldn't otherwise because of incompatible interfaces (Gamma et al., 1994).

Example: Many of the patterns require a consistent interface while implementation is allowed to vary. The *strategy* (see p. 50 of this book) is a good example. If such a pattern is used, then client objects are designed to that interface, allowing for additional implementations to be added in the future without changes to the clients (following open-closed). If a new implementation is provided, perhaps a purchased component or an implementing class provided by another team, then it may not fit into the existing pattern. An adapter can be added to solve this problem.

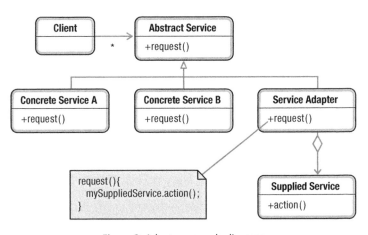

Figure 2: Adapter example diagram.

Qualities and Principles: The adapter class only changes the interface. Clients couple only to the original interface and never to the real interface of the foreign (supplied) object. Adapters contain no redundant implementation with existing components. The actual component, its real interface, and the fact that it is "foreign" is hidden from clients. Adapters preserve existing open-closed relationships and create substitutability with entities that are *conceptually* the same but cannot be *practically* treated the same. The adapter separates the concern of the real interface from the needed behavior.

Testing: An adapter can be tested using a mock object (see p. 38) in place of the supplied/foreign component.

Questions and Concerns: The adapter requires that the adapted component be fully capable. If it lacks some of the functionality that the local components have, then behavior(s) will have to be added to it. This can be done with either a proxy (see p. 46) or decorator (see p. 28).

The delta between the interfaces should be small. If it is not, it may be that a facade (see p. 30) is more appropriate.

The adapter is typically implemented as a kind of "wrapper" that delegates to the foreign component (as shown). However, it can be implemented using inheritance when greater performance is needed. This requires multiple inheritances or a language that supports other abstract types, like interfaces and delegates.

For more information: https://tinyurl.com/y6nkmdf6

The Bridge

Intent: The intent is to separate a varying *entity* from its varying *behavior*, so that the two can vary independently.

Another way to state it: The *bridge* is one variation using another variation in a varying way.

Example: One common use of the bridge is in data access frameworks. The varying entities would be elements of the system that need to access data in different ways (sequentially, random access, etc.). The varying behaviors would be the different data sources that actually store, retrieve, delete, and update data in different ways.

The idea is to be able to add new data consumers or new data providers without this affecting the other in each case. This makes the system open-closed to a new consumer, a new provider, or both.

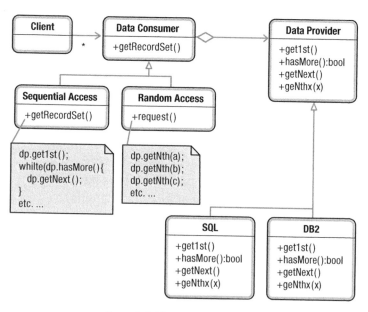

Figure 3: Bridge example diagram.

Qualities and Principles: Entities only consume and behaviors only provide, yielding strong cohesion and separation of concerns. The entities couple only to the behavioral interface. Clients couple only to the entity interface. Any potential redundancies can be pushed up to abstract base classes. Entities and behaviors, and the way entities use behaviors, are all hidden from the rest of the system. As a result, new entities and new behaviors can be added to the system, including new entities that use the behaviors in a new way, with little or no change to existing code.

Testing: Testing the behaviors is straightforward, as they have no dependencies. Testing an entity requires a mock behavior (see p. 38).

Questions and Concerns: Adding a new behavior is usually straightforward, unless the new behavior in question is lacking capability (or capabilities). If so, a proxy (see p. 46) or decorator (see p. 28) can be used to add the needed functionality.

Adding a new entity is also usually straightforward, unless the new entity requires something of the behaviors that is not currently in the interface. When this occurs, the interface of the behaviors must be changed, and thus all existing behaviors must be updated as well. This should be kept in mind as a potential maintenance issue.

The bridge requires that all behaviors have the same interface. If this is not true, then typically an adapter (see p. 18) or facade (see p. 30) is used to correct this.

For more information: https://tinyurl.com/y2vox7px

The Builder

Intent: Separate the construction of a complex object from its representation so the same construction process can create different representations (Gamma et al., 1994).

Example: A relational database contains information that can be consumed in different ways, depending on the needs of the client. Whereas one client might prefer to iterate over the data in a flat structure (like a Vector or ArrayList), another might need to see the data's parent-child relationships implied by the foreign keys that records contain (which link them to other tables) in the composite pattern (see p. 26). A builder would hide the details of construction, allowing the clients to specify which form of the data was desired without coupling to the specific steps required to make it.

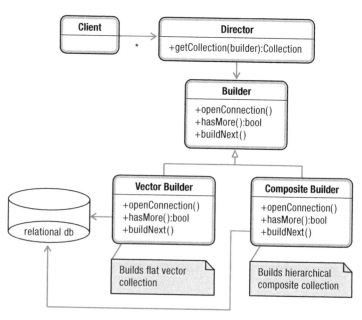

Figure 4: Builder example diagram.

Qualities and Principles: Each builder has the single responsibility of building a specific version of the complex object that is needed. Clients couple to the interface of the director, but not the builders. A client is only concerned with the builder that applies to its needs. The other builders, their specifics, and their number are not referenced by a given client, and thus the design is open-closed to new builders that make new versions of the complex object. The director interface comes from the needs of the clients. The builder interface comes from the nature of the object being built.

Testing: The director can be tested using a mock (see p. 38) of the builder interface. Each individual builder can be tested in a straightforward way, the specifics depending on the nature of the complex object being built. For example, to determine how to test the composite builder, one would refer to the composite pattern (see p. 26).

Questions and Concerns: There are different ways for the director to obtain the correct builder. The client may supply it, or the director may determine this based on the context of the application, etc. Sometimes another factory is used by the director to accomplish this. These issues must be dealt with on a case-by-case basis, as the nature of the problem domain will dictate what is correct in a given context. Because the different builders operate in sometimes vastly different ways, the performance of each may be inconsistent.

For more information: https://tinyurl.com/y3nmbkca

The Chain of Responsibility

Intent: Avoid coupling the sender of a request to its receiver by giving more than one object a chance to handle the request. Chain the receiving objects and pass the request along the chain until an object handles it (Gamma et al., 1994).

Example: A provider of retirement accounts and mutual funds could provide a web-based service allowing their customers to check on the current status of their investments on demand. The customers would be interested in knowing the most up-to-date information on how the stocks, bonds, and other instruments in their fund are currently priced by the market.

If there are several strategic partners that might be able to resolve a given financial symbol and "the right one" might change unpredictably, a chain of responsibility could be implemented to allow the request to flow from one provider to another until the answer is found.

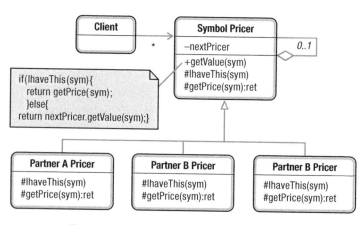

Figure 5: Chain of responsibility example diagram.

Qualities and Principles: Each member of the chain is focused on one version of the request. The clients are coupled only to the service interface. The number of services, their implementation details, how they are selected, and the order in which they are given a chance to handle the request are all encapsulated. New services can seamlessly be added, removed, and reordered within the chain. All potential redundancies can be pulled up into the base class. Dependencies between the services (e.g., service Y should only be attempted if service X does not apply) are inherently captured in the ordering of the chain.

Testing: Tests can be made subclasses of the service objects. Each service object can have two tests: one proving the object selects when it should, and another proving the selected behavior is correctly implemented. The ordering of the chain can be tested against the factory that builds it.

Questions and Concerns: What should happen if none of the objects in the chain can complete the request? This is a decision to be made on a case-by-case basis and should be considered early in the design process. The typical implementation of the chain of responsibility is a linked list, but, in fact, any collection can be used and scanned in any way desired. A template method (see p. 54), `getValue()` in the example, is typically used to implement this pattern internally to keep the "next" pointer private and to avoid redundantly implementing the "handoff to the next object" action.

For more information: https://tinyurl.com/yyfdbko5

The Composite

Intent: We want to handle items that are hierarchically related (either through classification or like a bill of materials) as objects.

Example: The most common example of a composite is a hierarchical file system. Files are placed into folders, but folders can also contain other folders to any desired depth. The purpose of such a composite is organizing (collecting files and folders that belong together), finding (the structure can be navigated in a search), and eliminating name collision (many folders in a file system can contain a file named README.TXT, for example, with no naming collision).

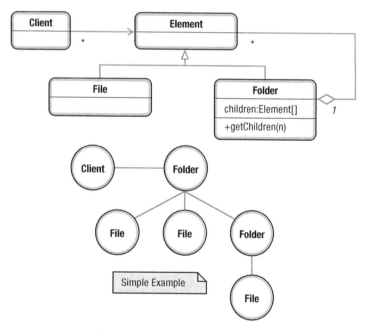

Figure 6: Composite example diagram.

Qualities and Principles: Simple and complex structures can be modeled with no change to design. Clients couple to the interface but implementation can be hidden from them. The responsibilities of leaf (file) and node (folder) are singular and separate. Leaf and node objects can be stored and retrieved interchangeably in many cases.

Testing: Leaf objects can be tested individually. Node objects can be tested using mock leaf objects (see p. 38).

Questions and Concerns: Composites come in two general forms: classification (as in the example) and bill of materials. The latter is used to model complex entities (e.g., a budget contains categories, the categories contain line items, the line items contain details). Summing the categories might be the desired behavior.

One decision that must be addressed is whether—and to what degree—to expose the difference between leaf objects and node objects to clients. Leaf objects do not contain other elements, whereas node objects do. If this difference is exposed to clients (a node would have methods like `getChild(n)` in the example, where a leaf would not), then this allows clients to traverse the structure but breaks the encapsulation of type. The correct balance of these factors is determined based on the purpose of the composite in a given problem domain.

Varying node/leaf behavior can be accomplished with the visitor (see p. 56) without breaking type encapsulation.

For more information: https://tinyurl.com/y3unzs7o

The Decorator

Intent: Attach additional responsibilities to an object dynamically. Decorators provide a flexible alternative to subclassing for extending functionality (Gamma et al., 1994).

Example: Processing an image for display or to send to a printer can involve many different manipulations depending on the effect desired and the capabilities (color gamut, etc.) of the target device.

These manipulations can include spatial passes, Fourier transformations, affine transformations, and so forth. Each does something different to alter the way the image appears. Once filtered, the image is displayed or printed.

An image processing system should allow for none, one, some, or all of these manipulations to be applied, and in any order desired by the end user.

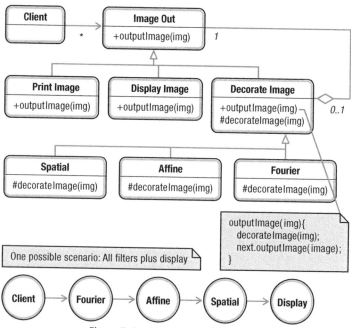

Figure 7: Decorator example diagram.

Qualities and Principles: Each decorator does a single kind of decoration, making them strongly cohesive. The clients couple only to the interface of the abstraction (`ImageOut` in the example). Which decorators are in use, the order in which they operate, and the final destination are all encapsulated from clients, and thus all are open-closed. The interface comes from no particular implementation, but from the clients' needs.

Testing: Each decorator can be tested using a mock of the decorated object to ensure it adds the proper decoration to the data it has passed, and that it passes on to the next object.

Questions and Concerns: Ideally, all decorators and the decorated objects should have the same interface to allow for maximum flexibility. An *adapter* (see p. 18) can be used when this is not true. A *decorator* is typically implemented using a template method (see p. 54) to separate the decorating behavior from the common handoff to the next behavior (the `OutputImage()` method in the example is a template method).

Decorator chains nearly always have business rules regarding which combinations are permissible and which are not, including constraints on sequence, and which decorators can and cannot be used together. Because of this, some kind of creational (factory) pattern is typically used to capture and enforce these restrictions and to separate them from client concerns.

For more information: https://tinyurl.com/yy3ur56t

The Facade

Intent: Provide a unified interface to a set of interfaces in a subsystem. *Facade* defines a higher level interface that makes the subsystem easier to use (Gamma et al., 1994).

Example: When planning a vacation, business trip, or other travel, there are a lot of different aspects that has to be reserved, scheduled, and otherwise arranged for. Each of these elements (a hotel, a rental car, etc.) has a different way of accessing them. In the past, this would involve a lot of phone calls, the use of a legacy system called Saber, some faxes, etc. People often preferred to use a travel agent to handle all of these details.

Conceptually, a travel agent is a facade: one person to deal with who hides all the complexity of the various interactions involved. They may even do things that we do not know are needed. Today, there are web-based services that do the same, and they are also an example of the facade pattern. They present a single interface that encapsulates all of the varying interfaces involved.

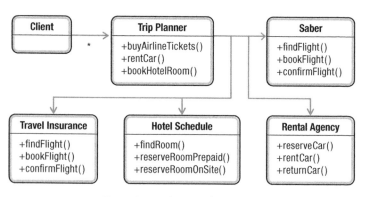

Figure 8: Facade example diagram.

Qualities and Principles: The facade decouples all clients from the various interfaces and types that it encapsulates, and how those types are designed and created. The interface of the facade is not based on any service implementation, but on the general needs of the clients that use it. The facade separates the concerns of use from all other concerns, simplifying and focusing clients.

Testing: The facade itself can be mocked, making the testing of all clients fundamentally simpler and faster. Testing the facade itself depends on the nature of the elements it encapsulates—how they are designed.

Questions and Concerns: Facades can end up being fairly heavyweight in terms of their memory footprint and instantiation time, so it is usually best if multiple instances of the facade are not needed. This means the facade should not become specialized for a particular client, and thus should contain no client-specific state. A *flyweight* (see p. 32) can be used to prevent this, and making the facade a *singleton* (see p. 48) can enforce that there is only one facade created. Once the facade interface is created, *adapters* (see p. 18) can be used for varying client needs.

Facades are often used when developing new code that has dependencies on legacy code. If a facade is introduced between new development and legacy, then the legacy nature (which may be highly procedural and/or low quality) does not influence/pollute new work. Facades also make legacy refactoring less risky.

For more information: https://tinyurl.com/y5x6kzos

The Flyweight

Intent: Use sharing to support large numbers of fine-grained objects efficiently (Gamma et al., 1994).

Example: Font systems model each letter with a different class that is capable of scaling, micropositioning, kerning, and other (often heavyweight) behaviors. If a large document contains many examples of, say, the letter A, then creating an instance of A for each appearance would be wasteful since all A's would behave the same; the only difference would be their location (row and column, for example). The *flyweight* suggests pulling out the varying state position into lightweight objects, all of which defer to the single instance of the letter for all behaviors.

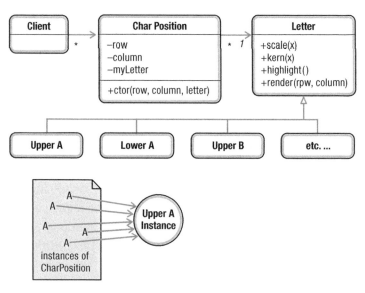

Figure 9: Flyweight example diagram.

Qualities and Principles: The flyweight is a quintessential example of the separation of concerns. The varying state is one concern; the consistent behavior is another. Clients couple only to the state object, never the behavior, whereas the state object couples to the abstraction of the behavior (`Letter` in the example). Any number of state objects can exist without requiring more behavior objects, eliminating redundant resource consumption.

Testing: The flyweight (`CharPosition` in the example) can easily be tested against a mock (see p. 38) of the behavioral object, making the test fast and narrowly focused.

Questions and Concerns: The flyweight increases delegation in the system to reduce resource consumption, but does create more use of the stack, the virtual access table (VAT), and other virtualization resources of the runtime. Thus, we sacrifice a bit of performance to avoid wasting memory.

The flyweight can be used to eliminate any manner of a client-specific state from coupling to any kind of behavior, thus whenever a heavyweight entity is created, the flyweight should be considered as a possibility. A good example of this is the facade (see p. 30).

The flyweight assumes that all reuse of the behavior object is consistent. If there are exceptions to this, an adapter (see p. 16) or proxy (see p. 46) can be used to resolve the differences. The behavior objects are often singletons (see p. 48) to enforce they are not created repeatedly.

For more information: https://tinyurl.com/y42bp2ru

The Mediator

Intent: Define an object that encapsulates how a set of objects interacts. A *mediator* promotes loose coupling by keeping objects from referring to each other explicitly, and it lets you vary their interaction independently (Gamma et al., 1994).

Example: Modern development tools often offer drag-and-drop mechanisms for creating graphical user interfaces, database connections, and other system elements. It is unadvisable to embed business logic in the code these tools generate, as it becomes difficult to test, reuse, and modify. A mediator can be introduced to encapsulate all coupling between the generated code and the handcrafted application logic. The mediator contains only the "wiring" between these elements. The elements do not couple to each other directly in any way.

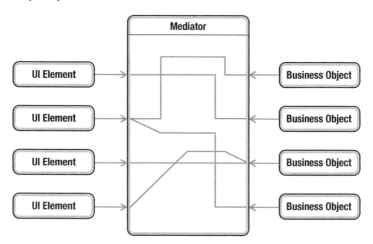

Figure 10: Mediator example diagram.

Qualities and Principles: The mediator fundamentally promotes decoupling in the system. It only contains connection logic, nothing more, and thus is strongly cohesive. The interface of the mediator is derived from the needs of the rest of the system, which are its clients. The mediator also promotes reuse and eliminates all potential redundancies in connection logic.

Testing: The mediator itself is a candidate for creating a mock (see p. 38), allowing for easier testing of all the elements that couple to it. Testing the mediator itself is an integration issue, and thus it will be tested less frequently than other parts of the system.

Questions and Concerns: Because the mediator can only be tested in integration, care should be taken to ensure that it does not contain complex failure modes. Ideally, the mediator should have no significant application logic beyond dispatching requests.

If flexible connections are needed, the observer (see p. 44) can be used when implementing the mediator.

If any significant logic is required (caching or remoting dispatches, etc.), then a proxy (see p. 46) should be used to add it, making it testable as a separate issue.

Mediators can serve as a kind of "application roadmap" since all events, requests, and services are routed through it. The more readable and clear its code is, the better it will serve this useful role.

For more information: https://tinyurl.com/y4nd6gjk

The Memento

Intent: Without violating encapsulation, capture and externalize an object's internal state so that the object can be restored to this state later (Gamma et al., 1994).

Example: Sometimes it is necessary to take a point-in-time "snapshot" of an object so that it can be temporarily changed and then later restored to the original condition. This means that the state of the object must be able to be recorded and then restored. If the state in question is encapsulated (a best practice), then this would seem to be a challenge. How can we extract that which cannot be read? How can we restore that which cannot be written? The *memento* solves this problem.

The stateful object in question is typically called "the originator." The object that captures the state is the memento. The memento must have a more intimate relationship to the originator than the rest of the system. There are many ways to accomplish this. In the example below, a narrow interface is used. Other implementations are possible depending on the technology being used.

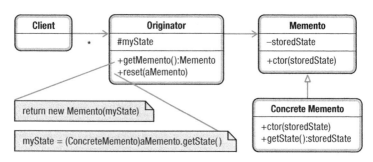

Figure 11: Memento example diagram.

Qualities and Principles: The memento allows us to preserve the encapsulation of state, even under circumstances that would seem to dictate breaking it. The memento object is strongly cohesive in that it only stores state, nothing else. The interface of the originator is derived from the client's need to take a snapshot of the state. The `ConcreteMemento` (in the example) is substitutable for the memento that the client is exposed to, allowing the interface to vary in a way that is hidden to all clients.

Testing: The memento is an enabler for testing in that it allows a test to take an object through various scenarios and then return it to its original condition.

Testing that the memento accurately restores the state can be accomplished by making the test the *originator*, or by making it a subclass of the originator. The latter approach requires the state to be protected rather than private.

Questions and Concerns: The memento in the example does not literally enforce encapsulation in that a client object could, theoretically, downcast the reference in the same way that the originator does. If this is a concern, then the `ConcreteMemento` may be made package-private, or may be an inner class of the originator if the technology supports this idiom. Other possibilities exist, including the use of delegates or assembly metadata in .Net, etc.

For more information: https://tinyurl.com/y5hc4yo6

The Mock Object

Intent: When a unit being tested has a dependency, replace that dependency with a version that is only for testing, called a *mock object*. The mock object can be conditioned and inspected by the test.

Example: An application makes use of a *web service* through an access object to obtain some critical information as part of its implementation. When testing the application, actually accessing the web service will make the test too slow and/or will produce results that the test cannot predict. Also, it is not certain the web service will always be available when the test is running.

The web service access object is replaced with a mock that is predictable, fast, and guaranteed. The test can determine what the mock will return and inspect if (and how) the application accessed it.

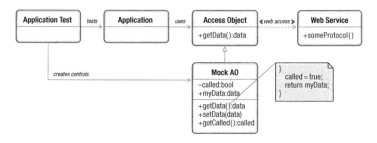

Figure 12: Mock object example diagram.

*Note: This is only **one way** to create mock; in this case, using direct inheritance (which may not always be desirable). There are many other ways, any of which could be preferable depending on circumstances.*

Qualities and Principles: The mock replaces a dependency, controlling coupling for the purpose of testing. The test's concern (application logic) is separated from the concern of the dependency, allowing the test to narrowly focus on the behavior it specifies. The interface of the mock is based on client need, as the test takes the same position as a client would/will. The mock is substitutable for the original dependency from the client point of view. The need/desire to make mocking possible in testing scenarios promotes the open-closed principle, as mocks must be introduced without changes to application logic.

Testing: The mock enables the test of the application under test. Mocks are inherently controllable by their own tests as well.

Questions and Concerns: There are many ways of creating mocks, including the use of a mock object framework to automate their production. Mocks should be kept as simple as possible to avoid excessive testing scenarios involving them. Mocks should not be public objects; they should be available only to test code and should be part of a test project or namespace.

Additionally, it must be decided how to replace the real dependency with the mock version while the test is running. This can be accomplished in various ways, including the use of a dependency injection framework.

For more information: https://tinyurl.com/yy7rv8lz

The Null Object

Intent: Rather than using a null reference when an object is absent, create an object that implements the expected interface but whose methods have no behavior.

Many of the behavioral design patterns such as *state* (see p. 52) and *strategy* (see p. 50) allow implementation to vary without specializing clients. Often when a behavior or algorithm has many different versions, one of those versions may be to have no behavior at all. To avoid using special-case conditional code (e.g., if (!null)), into clients, a *null object* can be used.

Example: A system sends messages over a network socket. Sometimes these messages need to be encrypted in various ways, depending on the client and/ or receiver involved. The *strategy pattern* is used to hide this variation from the socket class. However, there are times when the data should be sent in clear text, with no encryption applied at all. A *null encrypter* can be used when this is appropriate.

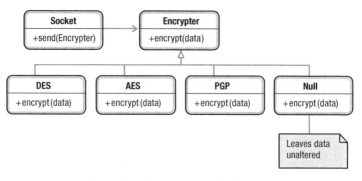

Figure 13: Null object example diagram.

Qualities and Principles: *Null object* eliminates null pointer checks in client objects—code which would otherwise be redundant. The *fact* that the algorithm in question is optional is *encapsulated*, which means it may not be optional in the future (making it open-closed) without any changes to clients. Null objects are substitutable for all other versions of the behavior in question.

Testing: Typically, a null object requires no test since it has no behavior. However, a simple test may be written to ensure no behavior is inadvertently added to the object in the future, and/or to capture (as a specification) that the behavior is an optional one.

Questions and Concerns: A null object must have the same interface as the other implementations, but it is advisable to name parameters in such a way as to make it clear they are not used, like `m(ignoreData d)` or code to that effect. When a null object is used then the delegation from the clients to the service object is always made (it is reliable). Whenever there are reliable points of delegation from one object to another, this becomes an integration point for new behavior, which often leads to the *proxy pattern* (see p. 46). Also, in the *chain of responsibility* (see p. 24), one issue that must be resolved is what should be done if none of the potential service objects "elects" itself. It may be appropriate to put a null object at the end of the chain.

For more information: https://tinyurl.com/y4zlrdqo

The Object Pool

Intent: Create a manager class to represent a pool of reusable resources. Clients will access the manager to obtain an instance of the resource and return it when their task is complete.

Example: Connections are to be made to a data resource on a server. The *server* will allow from 1 to 255 connections to be made. If one connection is made, then clients must wait for the connection to be available, but the server's performance will be fast. If 255 connections are made, then clients need not wait for an available connection, but the server will bog down servicing so many connections. It is unpredictable what the best balance point is for optimal throughput.

An *object pool* could be used to manage a set of reusable connection objects. The number of objects is encapsulated and thus easy to change.

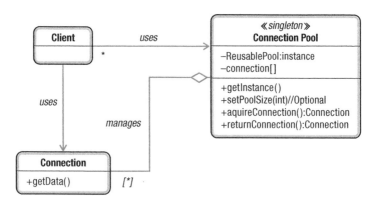

Figure 14: Object pool example diagram.

Qualities and Principles: The *object pool* separates the concerns of use from creation, but also the nature of the pool itself. How many objects are in it, if they are reused or remade each time, if they are used by more than one client (load-balanced), all these things are encapsulated and therefore easily changeable. The managed objects are substitutable for each other.

Testing: Testing the manager itself is fairly straightforward:

- Tests can be written to ensure the proper object type is created, that the manager blocks when it should, etc.
- If the pool collection is given protected access, a unit test can subclass the manager and thus observe the size of the pool under different scenarios.
- Testing the managed objects depends on their nature and design. Often, they are designed using other patterns.

Questions and Concerns: One decision that must always be addressed with the object pool is whether or not to make the pool size dynamic. The `setPoolSize(int)` method is optional and should only be added if changing the pool size will not violate any system contracts, and if different application contexts will require it. The default option is to keep the pool size static.

For more information: https://tinyurl.com/y6jrmbhv

The Observer

Intent: Define a one-to-many dependency between objects so that when one object changes state, all its dependents are notified and updated automatically (Gamma et al., 1994).

Example: An object is created to represent the current session of a logged-in user at a web service. Other parts of the system need to know when the session ends—and whether that is because the user has logged out, the session has timed out, the connection has failed, or any other reason. It's also important to note the length of time the session was active at the moment it expires.

The *observer* would allow any part of the system that was "interested" to sign up for the notification.

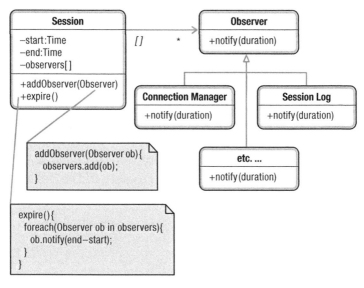

Figure 15: Observer example diagram.

Qualities and Principles: The observed object is decoupled from the observers—both their nature and number. Each observer has a different, single reason to sign up for notifications. The design is open-closed to new observers.

Testing: A test can use a *mock observer* (see p. 38) to record what happens when the event in question is triggered. Each observer can be triggered by the test calling the `notify()` method, and then tested depending on the nature of the observer (how it is designed).

Questions and Concerns: If all observers need the same information when the event occurs (as is true in the example), then the `notify()` method can be parameterized. If, on the other hand, different observers need different information, this can be accomplished two ways:

1) The observed object can pass a reference to itself, allowing each observer to call back in different ways.

2) An association object can be created and populated with all information that could possibly be required, and each observer can retrieve whatever it needs.

The observers and the observed objects might be in different process threads, or on different ends of a network connection. A proxy (see p. 46) can be used to cache events to improve performance if needed, or to add the remoting behavior if only some observers are remote.

For more information: https://tinyurl.com/yxqggxhq

The Proxy

Intent: Add *some* functionality to an existing object externally in such a way that neither the client nor the service objects need to change.

Example: Financial institutions (banks, saving and loans, etc.) maintain accounts for their customers, sometimes using objects. These *account* objects are used for transaction processing, reporting, in the ATM and teller software, etc. Sometimes an audit trace needs to be placed on a given account if, for example, it has been overdrawn excessively. This "trace" behavior is added when appropriate, and removed when the issue is resolved. A proxy can be used to add the tracing.

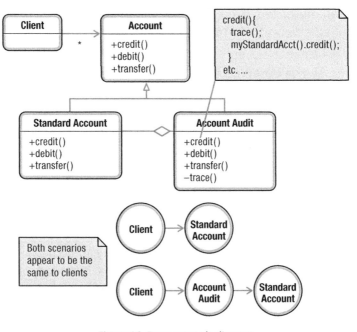

Figure 16: Proxy example diagram.

Qualities and Principles: The proxy is focused on adding a single behavior, making it cohesive. It also preserves the cohesion of the original object since the additional behavior is added externally. It does not redundantly implement the behavior of the original object; it reuses it.

Clients that couple to the interface of the original object do not change when the proxy is added, following open-closed. The interface for the proxy is the same as the original; if that interface followed dependency inversion, the proxy preserves this fact. The proxy is substitutable for the original and encapsulates the fact that two objects are in play rather than one.

Testing: The proxy can be tested using a mock (see p. 38) of the original object.

Questions and Concerns: The proxy can be used to add *any* kind of behavior that does not require a change to the original interface: asynchrony, security, caching, remoting, logging, etc. The proxy can create inconsistent performance in that, when it is used, a double dispatch will take place rather than a single. If this is a concern, the proxy can be implemented by subclassing the original class, though this does have limitations of its own. The proxy only adds behavior; it does not alter the interface. If the interface needs changing, the proxy is often paired with the *adapter* (see p. 18). Proxy often evolves over time into a *decorator* (see p. 28) when multiple added behaviors are needed due to new requirements.

For more information: https://tinyurl.com/y2tl6o34

The Singleton

Intent: Ensure a class only has one instance and provide a global point of access to it (Gamma et al., 1994).

Example: A system allows a single user to log in at a time. The currently logged-in user is represented by an object—an instance of a *user* class—that contains all the information needed throughout the system about the user, including their access level, their rights, permissions in the system, etc.

Different parts of the system will need access to this object to determine what this particular user should be allowed to do or to view, which elements should or should not appear on a menu in the user interface (UI), which parts of the database should be made available, etc.

The instance could be passed to every part of the system that needs access to it, but this can be laborious, error prone, and can produce potential redundancies. If it is made a *singleton* instead, then any part of the system that needs access to it will cleanly retrieve it for itself.

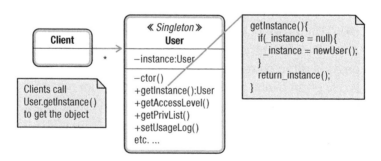

Figure 17: Singleton example diagram.

Qualities and Principles: The *singleton* aspect of an object ensures there is only one instance, reflecting the needs of clients to interact with a shared resource. Although the typical singleton is concrete, there is no coupling to this fact in clients; if it evolves into an abstract type over time, only the static `getInstance()` method must change because the singleton avoids redundant construction logic in the system.

Testing: A unit test can call `getInstance()` twice and assert that the object obtained is the same both times.

Questions and Concerns: Since any part of the system can obtain the same instance of the singleton, care must be taken to ensure that it contains no state that can be both read and written. If one part of the system can read the state and another can write it, then this creates uncontrolled coupling much as a global variable would.

The singleton is not inherently thread safe. When `getInstance()` is called for the first time, the creation of the instance takes time to complete, and if a second thread enters the method during this period, a second instance could result. Locking the method is one way to alleviate this, but there are other options (see below).

Facades (see p. 30) are often singletons since they tend to be heavyweight objects, and we may want to enforce that they are not built before needed and are never built multiple times.

For more information: https://tinyurl.com/yyb6p8b7

The Strategy

Intent: Define a family of algorithms, encapsulate each one, and make them interchangeable. Strategy lets the algorithm vary independently from clients that use it (Gamma et al., 1994).

Example: Businesses purchase various equipment, properties, vehicles, and so forth as required to operate. The cost of these "assets" can be deducted from the profits of the business, reducing their tax liability.

However, it is not permissible to "write off" the entire value of an asset immediately; it must be done gradually over time using an algorithm for what is termed "fixed asset amortization." There are various algorithms for doing this; the right one depends on a number of factors: type of asset, which governmental entity is being reported to, where it was purchased, etc.

Amortization is often "capped" at a maximum and is dependent on a "business domain" code from the General Services Administration (GSA).

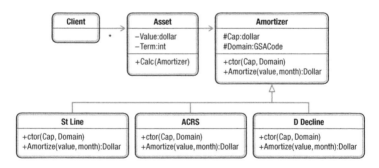

Figure 18: Strategy example diagram.

Qualities and Principles: Each *strategy* object is responsible for one version of the algorithm and is thus cohesive. Any potentially redundant elements can be pulled up into the base class. Clients couple only to the strategy interface; all specific algorithm implementations are encapsulated and open-closed. Strategy objects are substitutable for one another. The interface of the strategy is derived from client need, not from any particular implementation. Strategy separates the concern of the algorithm from all other concerns.

Testing: Each *strategy* implementation can be tested on its own. The *context* object (asset, in the example) can be tested using a mock (see p. 38) of the strategy interface.

Questions and Concerns: Strategy adds a virtual method call to the system, which can impede performance. It removes all *intimacy* between the algorithm and the state which it operates on; the state must be passed in/back.

Strategy requires all versions of the algorithm to have the same interface and to be castable to the same base type. If this is not true, an adapter (see p. 18) can be used to resolve this.

Strategy allows all versions of an algorithm to be used interchangeably. If there are business rules about which version should be used and under what circumstances, another pattern must be used to enforce them: typically, one of the creational patterns, depending on the domain.

For more information: https://tinyurl.com/y2q5gdep

The State

Intent: The system needs to behave differently when it is in various conditions (*states*). This often occurs when a program is modal.

Example: The software in an ATM is operated by the end user through an interface that has various buttons and a keypad for entering numbers. The buttons will do various things depending on where the user is in the workflow. A given button might be used to select "withdraw funds" and then that same button might be subsequently used to select which account to withdraw from. Similarly, the keypad that allowed the user to enter their PIN could be used later to enter the amount of a deposit.

The *state pattern* could be used to manage these changes. As the system is used, the state object is changed and thus all behaviors transition to the appropriate versions.

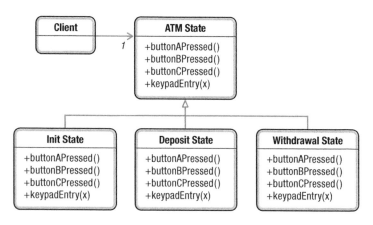

Figure 19: State example diagram.

Qualities and Principles: Each state object encapsulates the behaviors that are appropriate for one mode of the system, making them easier to understand and change. The clients couple only to the state interface, which is derived from the nature of their needs. All state objects are interchangeable with one another. If there are common behaviors (`exitKeyPressed()` in the example), these can be implemented in the base class, avoiding redundancies. New states can be added and/or existing states removed with little or no impact on clients.

Testing: Each state object can be tested on its own through its public interface. The client can be tested using a mock (see p. 38) of the state interface.

Questions and Concerns: One issue that must always be resolved is how the transitions from state to state are to be handled. This will change based on the context of the domain, but some possibilities include:

- Each state object, when used, can return the appropriate next state object. This does tend to couple them to each other, however.
- A routine in the client can contain the logic to change states. Care is needed to prevent redundancies if multiple clients require the same or similar logic.
- A state manager class can be used by all clients to manage these transitions.

For more information: https://tinyurl.com/y3kqgn85

The Template Method

Intent: We want to abstract out a common theme from different cases that have different implementations of an algorithm.

Example: Often systems/frameworks have a fixed workflow where the steps are always executed in a specific sequence, but the actions taken in each step vary by application context. *Template method* separates the common workflow from the individual steps it executes/organizes. The template method may also contain common conditionals or other logic that does not vary by implementation.

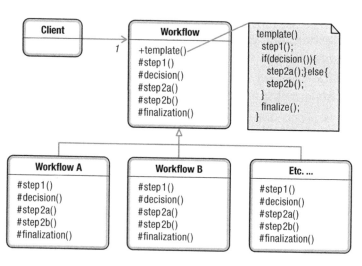

Figure 20: Template method example diagram.

A Conceptual Diagram

Qualities and Principles: The template method separates a common workflow from its varying implementations. The workflow is not redundantly implemented, and each implementation is about one version of the process. All implementations are interchangeable. The interface of the template method is derived from the needs of clients. The template method encapsulates the workflow itself, the varying implementations (their number and nature), and which are currently active, making them open-closed.

Testing: The template method (Workflow, in the example) can be tested using a mock implementation (see p. 38) that can capture and record how it is used to ensure its methods are called correctly. Each implementation (`WorkflowA`, etc., in the example) can have its own test; if protected methods are used, the test can be made a subclass in each case.

Questions and Concerns: The template method is intended to abstract out the steps of an *algorithm*. If the steps are actually different algorithms, then the template method may have weak cohesion. When this is the case, the step methods to correct this should delegate to behavioral objects rather than embedding the code in the actual implementation class. If this is done, then the "single algorithm" would be the workflow itself.

Many patterns have template method as part of their implementation: decorator (see p. 28) and chain of responsibility (see p. 24) are typical examples.

For more information: https://tinyurl.com/y5c3faea

The Visitor

Intent: Set up a structure that allows the addition of operations across a variety of classes without changing the classes.

Example: A system that allows for the drawing of primitive, vector-based graphical objects (*shapes*) might need to allow for various transformational operations to be performed on these shapes, where the nature of the operation would vary based on which shape it is applied to. To "expand" a rectangle, for instance, involves multiplying its corners by a given factor. To "expand" a circle means to increase its radius. To "rotate" a square involves sine and cosine (sin and cos) calculations (trigonometry). To "rotate" a circle probably does nothing.

The *visitor* would allow for these operations to be extensible; additional kinds of transformations could be added without having to change the design of the shape objects.

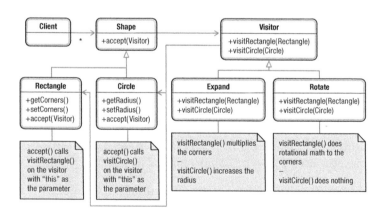

Figure 21: Visitor example diagram.

Qualities and Principles: The *visitor* enables open-closedness where the operations are concerned. Each visitor object is about one set of operations. The visited objects (*shapes*, in the example) are also strongly cohesive; they are only responsible for selecting the correct method to call on the visitor. Clients do not couple to specific visitors or specific visited objects. The `accept(Visitor)` method they call is established at the abstract level, and takes an abstraction as its only parameter. All visitors and visited objects are thus interchangeable.

Testing: Both the visitor and the visited objects can be tested by using a mock (see p. 38) of the opposite interface.

- The test of a visitor would ensure that the operations performed are correct in each case.
- The test of a visited object would ensure it calls the correct method on the visitor interface.

Questions and Concerns: This design allows for the addition of new visitors very cleanly. It does not allow for the easy addition of visited objects, however, as the visitor interface is dependent on the specific types that currently exist in the visited structure. Adding to that structure would require maintenance of all existing visitors. This is not a "failing of the pattern"; it is simply a reality. In the example, adding a new shape will require determining how to perform each existing transformation upon it.

For more information: https://tinyurl.com/y52orvko

Practice: Programming by Intention

Programming by intention (PBI) is a way of writing code that capitalizes on the way a programmer thinks.

Whenever you write code, what you are essentially doing is breaking down a behavior into its steps. In a sense, that's what code is. So your brain, as a developer, is good at this. PBI says let's capitalize on that fact.

For example, you have a transaction processor that can commit a transaction more than one way, depending on its size. The transaction string needs to be tokenized and normalized before being committed. PBI suggests you write the code thusly:

```
class Transaction {
 public Boolean commit(String command){
  Boolean result = true;
  String[] tokens = tokenize(command);
  normalizeTokens(tokens);
  if(tokens.Length > getMaximumLength()){
   result =
   processLargeTransaction(tokens);
  } else {
   result =
   processSmallTransaction(tokens);
  }
  return result;
 }
}
```

The methods in bold do not exist yet. We are hypothesizing that they will later: We will create them. This is a very simple thing to learn and do. But what is the point? Why is it a good idea?

The Value of Programming by Intention

Coding in this way creates a fundamental separation of concerns.

- The primary function code is all about the process of the behavior. If, in the example, this code is inherited by a new developer or team, then reading the `commit()` method in the example will tell the entire story of how this object works.

- Each helper method is about the implementation of one step along the way. This makes finding defects and integrating new steps much easier. It also makes the code easier to understand, thus requiring minimal comments along the way.

Also, creating discrete methods for each functional step makes for reusability and ease in refactoring. For example, if later it is determined that tokenizing the committed string should be done in different ways under different circumstances, then converting the `tokenize()` method into a strategy (see p. 30) will be much easier since the code is already isolated into a method.

Programming by intention can be adopted as a practice because it does not create additional work: The code written into the helper methods is the same code that would have been written in-line. It's just written at a different time and in a different location. It's not "more"; it's simply "different." Also, developers will readily adopt it once they try it even a single time. It proves itself.

Practice: Encapsulate Constructors in Simple Classes

A recurring question in object-oriented software (OO) is this: When it is determined that an algorithm should be established in its own separate class (to make it testable, reusable, or simply as an issue of cohesion), should it also be given a separate abstract type that it implements?

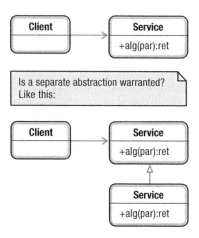

The advantage, of course, is that the client (or clients, as more arise) will not couple to the specific service class, but rather to the abstract type. If more versions of the service are added, then clients will be largely unaffected. It's a form of "future proofing." But can you do this all the time? Should every class, when deemed necessary, also have a second class that hides its real type? Often this would seem like overkill/overdesign. Does that mean it should never be done? That seems wrong too. So, is there something that can be done to resolve this conundrum?

The Encapsulating Constructors Practice

One very simple solution to this is to encapsulate the constructor of simple classes:

```
class Service {
 private Service() {}
 public static Service getInstance() {
  return new Service();
 }
 // rest of implementation follows
}
class Client {
 private Service myService;
 public Client() {
  // instead of "myService = new
  // Service();"
  myService = Service.getInstance();
 }
}
```

At first glance, this does not seem like much. Calling the static method getInstance() couples the client to the service type as much as using new does. The difference is that the latter couples the client to the fact that service is concrete, and the former does not. An abstract class can sport a static method just as well as a concrete class can. But new cannot be used on an abstract class.

This means that later, if needed, the service can be changed to this, with limited or no effect on any clients.

```
abstract class Service {
 public static Service getInstance() {
  // return any one of many
implementations
  // based on appropriate decision logic
 }
}
```

Practice: Encapsulate by Policy, Reveal by Need

Encapsulation has traditionally been thought of as the hiding of data, or "state." While it is true that hiding data encapsulates them, encapsulation can mean much more than this. It's like the notion that all dogs are mammals, but not all mammals are dogs.

Encapsulation is the hiding of anything. A lot of things can be encapsulated besides data.

For example:

- How something is designed
- How something is created
- When something is created
- The number of actions that take place
- The order in which actions take place
- The actual type of something
- The nature of a type (concrete or abstract)
- An interface
- The implementation of anything
- The structure of a collection
- The current status (mode) of a system
- The number of modes a system has
- The cause of a modal change
- etc.

Learning the patterns teaches you how to encapsulate all of these things, and more. But not everything should be encapsulated. How do we decide what to encapsulate once we know how?

The Value of Encapsulating by Policy

Knowing how to do something empowers you. But then you have to decide under what circumstances to do it and when not to.

This would make for a good sign to put on the wall where you'll see it repeatedly throughout your workday:

Encapsulate by policy, reveal by need.

Encapsulation is a decision. We know it is inevitable that we will make mistakes and will make wrong choices from time to time. The question is, what will we have to do when we realize we are in error?

If you encapsulate something and then realize later that you should not have (perhaps you need to make it reusable, or you need to test it in isolation, etc.), then breaking encapsulation is usually trivial. You either change it from a private thing to a public thing, or you add some kind of accessor, like a `get()` method. This is easy.

If, on the other hand, you *fail* to encapsulate something and then realize later that you should have, this can be a lot of work, especially if other parts of the system have become coupled to it over time. It can cause a redesign of those other parts. This can cause a lot of rework.

Encapsulating too much can be an easy problem to solve. Encapsulating too little is often very difficult to solve.

I'd rather make the mistake of encapsulating too much.

Practice: Adhere to a Coding Standard

One of the simplest practices a development team can benefit from is the adoption of a coding standard. Such a standard is simply a set of straightforward rules that everyone on the team agrees to. They include:

- **Naming conventions:** How variables, objects, functions, components, etc., are named
- **Structural choices:** How packages and namespaces are arranged, etc.
- **Lexicographical consistency:** Tabbing, placement of braces, capitalization
- **Terminology:** A set of domain terms that everyone knows, understands, and agrees on; these should also be agreed to by nontechnical parts of the organization (This is often called a domain-specific language, or DSL.)
- **etc.**

Each organization can and should decide what is important in the standard, and everyone must agree to adhere to it. It should also be easy to find and update: A wiki is one good solution for storing it.

These are not hard to follow; they are simple little choices that can become second nature over time.

If they are universally adopted, then everyone can read everyone else's code efficiently. This is essential for effective collaboration.

Acknowledgments

My personal understanding of good analysis, good design, and the patterns themselves has been enormously impacted by my association with a number of very smart and helpful colleagues. Among them are (alphabetically):

Sassan Azhadi

David Bernstein

Max Guernsey III

Amir Kolsky

Robert C. Myers

Alan Shalloway

James Trott

Also, several other authors, most of whom I do not know personally, have been essential to my development as a technology professional through their written work:

Christopher Alexander

Joshua Bloch

James O. Coplien

Bruck Eckel

Eric Freeman

The "Gang of Four" (GoF):

Erich Gamma, Richard Helm, Ralph Johnson, John Vlissides

Robert C. Martin

Robert M. Pirsig

Elisabeth Robson

Gerald Weinberg

Rebecca Wirfs-Brock

References

Alexander, C. (1979). *The timeless way of building*. Oxford University Press.

Dijkstra, E. W. (1982). "On the role of scientific thought." *Selected writings on Computing: A Personal Perspective* (pp. 60–66). Springer-Verlag.

Gamma, E., Helm, R., Johnson, R. E., & Vlissides, J. (1994). *Design patterns: Elements of reusable object oriented software*. Addison-Wesley.

Liskov, B., Wing, J. (1994). A behavioral notion of subtyping. *ACM Transactions on Programming Languages and Systems 16*(6), 1811–1841.

Martin, R. C. (2003). *Agile software development, principles, patterns, and practices*. Prentice Hall.

Meyer, B. (1988). *Object-oriented software construction*. Prentice Hall.

About the Author

Scott L. Bain is a 40-plus-year veteran in computer technology, with a background in development, engineering, and design. He has also designed, delivered, and managed training programs for certification and end-user skills, both in traditional classrooms and via distance learning. Mr. Bain teaches courses and consults on agile analysis and design patterns, advanced software design, and sustainable test-driven development.

He is a frequent speaker at developer conferences such as JavaOne and SDWest, and is the author of *Emergent Design*, which won a Jolt Productivity Award. He is also the author of *The TDD Companion* and is a co-author of *Essential Skills for the Agile Developer*.

Email: slbain9000@gmail.com

Personal blog: http://www.slbain.com

Pattern repository:
https://www.netobjectives.net/patternrepository